Beyond Bulrush

Beyond Bulrush

Jeannie E. Roberts

ISBN: 978-1-943170-11-1

Author Image: Elsa Statz

Cover Design: Jessica Smith

Original/Unaltered Cover Image: Leslie Raine Carman

Interior Design: Jessica Smith and Jane L. Carman

Production Director: Jane L. Carman

Typefaces: Garamond and Aguafina Script

Published by: Lit Fest Press, Carman, 688 Knox Road 900 North,
Gilson, Illinois 61436

L i t
Fest
Press

There are no rules.
festivalwriter.org

For my mom,
Karin Alice Smith Roberts
(1924 - 2013)

Contents

I. Holding Moments

II. Dimmer Switch

III. Natural Orbits

And everything that made me has been a sun to my growing. That is the article of my faith. Even the darkness of that soil that went before the light was another kind of sun.
—Rainer Maria Rilke, Bohemian-Austrian Poet
and Novelist (1875-1926)

I. Holding Moments

Along the Old Abe State Trail

Buoyant with the prospect of spring, buffleheads
float beside the drab fringe of April. Reeds rise
near water's edge, stand their ground weathered
in the beige remains of winter. Tree frogs fuse
with pitch and personality, resonate the essence
of old friends. Pine snake slithers through the
browns and buffs of withered grass as afternoon's
overcast dims the division between river and sky.
I rise near the Chippewa's edge, stand my ground
holding the bounty of another season about to unfold.

Gratitude

It's the heavenly sound
when chimes find a song
in breeze, the sparkle
of snow, the back and forth
show where hummingbirds
feed, it's an endless blue sky
when summer's not shy
to shine, the ferment
of leaves, the woodlands
at ease, in fall, it's the call
of a thrush when evening's
at hush in June, the echo
of grouse, the skitter
of mouse, near crocus
in bloom, it's the swoop
of an owl, the pitch
of its howl, in spring,
it's the high wire coos
on a walk where you choose
to love the life that you lead.

Front Porch

Forgiveness is the fragrance
that the violet sheds
on the heel that has crushed it.
—Mark Twain

In our sixty-three Chevy, under
a Minnesota moon, Dad drove
Snelling to Van Buren, where
the lights of St. Paul felt magical,
bright with possibilities as they
lit the way to Gram's boulevard,
to her three-season front porch.

"Not too wild now!" she'd holler.
My swing zigzags were a bit reckless.
Even so, I was careful long enough
to notice her tidy, little setting: two
corner stands with philodendrons,
four wicker chairs, freshly painted,
and a table, alive with the brightest,
most enchanting, African violets.

Now, in the fall of my life, under
a Wisconsin moon, where the stars
of Chippewa Falls feel magical,
glow over hills, meadows and the
unbridled beauty of wilderness,

I recall a wildflower, bright, alive,
crushed many times over while
trying to bloom, to fit, within all
the tidy, little settings. Even so,

I glide in the fragrance of forgiveness
and autumn's October air, moving
smoothly, without zigzag, on my
very own porch swing.

Adverbially Speaking, She's Not the Best Fit for a White Picket Fence

Preferably meadows
or grassy glades
decidedly wheat fields
or rolling waves

certainly oceans
indispensably seas
naturally nature
where freedom breathes

favorably forests
near glassy lakes
respectively rivers
where morning breaks

undoubtedly pastures
unquestionably breeze
naturally nature
where edges ease

primarily clear skies
where eagles glide
notably hoot owls
where echoes rise

Jeannie E. Roberts

(advisedly pickets
especially white
promise confinement
limits for life) so

preferably mountains
with neighboring streams
naturally nature
no fences please.

When Barred Owls Broadcast

There's hubbub,
hoopla, hobnob,
of a feathered sort,
ballyhoo in hoots
and hollers, stirring
birch, spinning
aspen, rising
from the ragged
tag and speckled
alders of Hallie.
Beneath beaks,
talons grip
atop lectern-like
limbs, where
proposals spring
off pulpit-shaped
boughs. With
persuasive pitch,
Strix varia hawks
its wares, boosts
the benefits of its
roosting hollows—
hootenanny style!
When weather
reports, hails
its hello's, derails
and drowns out
the show. In time,

static clears,
the broadcast
resumes and calls
go vernal, go viral again.

Four-Leafing
at Age Eight

In summer
when life
hummed
with a frenzy

when buzzing
brewed
over clover
when flowers

spilled
with the bumbling
of bees
she'd seek

with a purpose
hand-sweep
along surface
past purple

toward leaflets
of green.
Where wide
she'd patrol

comb valley
search knoll
knee-walk
bee talk

her way
all this
for a good luck
bouquet.

Berry Picking

—below the bluffs

We'd hold the stem
just above the fruit,
between forefinger

and thumb, pull
with a slight
twist, then grin

as each juicy
little jewel, red
with aroma, rolled

into our hands.
It was late June,
early mornings,

when we'd pick,
gather hearts
together,

at the Pepin
U-Pick-'Em
strawberry patch.

Butternuts

It was here,
near the stream,
under pinnate-shaped

leaves, where
she'd collect them,
where they'd amass

in her basket, brim
by the bushel. It was
here, in the Octobers

of her youth, beneath
the white walnut,
where she found hundreds

of butternuts. Some
fell in clusters, others
one by one. And now,

while she holds this memory,
she wonders, had she thought
to harvest the nuts

for candy, to boil
the rinds for dye?
Or perhaps

she'd been prompted
by an echo, answered
a ten-thousand-year-old

call. Whatever
the urge, clearly
she liked to collect,

to gather, as she did
fossils, four-leaf
clovers, rocks

and, later in life,
men, especially
the fallen ones,

the ones she deemed
in need of rescue—
quite like those

butternuts:
abundantly culled,
heedfully hulled,

only to discover
that most were rotten.
So, she threw them out.

Butterfly

Your order flew
through my door,
a class act

of *Insecta*—
full-blown,
four wings

fully grown,
a feast
for furtive eyes.

But before
you fluttered,
time was spent

unfolding,
inflating,
producing juice

for the journey.
There you waited,
defenseless,

tender to attack,
drying, until
your wide-eyed

wings let loose
on waves of air.
Lepidoptera:

you've lived
fourfold,
been altered,

reshaped, reborn
and now,
you've shown me,

through my door,
you're my life
in metaphor.

Art Fair

—near the shores

Down Great River Road,
past the family cottage
and clear-cut memories
of lighthearted days,

a train whistle blasts
and Saturday shines
as only the third

Saturday in July can.
At Stockholm's Village
Park, artists, musicians

and fair-goers merge,
fuse with the unity
of gathering, lighten
with the poetry of place.

An Earnest Fable

*Love is like a dew that falls
on both nettles and lilies.*
—Swedish Proverb

Covered in pine boughs and dew,
she awoke to drumming sounds.
Wings were the start of this day,
and hers began to unfold. As sun
slipped between cedars, it warmed
the forest floor. Fern unfurled
and bloodroot revealed its golden
center. Shaking her wings, she
blanketed the woodlands—*Mist de
Amor*, she called it. Gathering her
gusto, she set out to soften all the
thorns, nettles, and troublesome things,
scattering more dew as she flew.

Muguet

(Lily of the Valley in French)

It takes me back, that fragrance, the scent
of my mother. She smelled of sweetness
and crystalline light. And as I walk,

the essence of *muguet* lingers as reflections
of perfume bottles crystallize in my mind,
where delicate glass gatherings gleamed atop

her bedroom vanity. The Kosta Boda
with stopper was my favorite; its teardrop-
shape fit perfectly in my hand. I'd gaze into it

like a fortune teller with crystal ball.
I hold this imagery, absorb its sweetness,
as I walk the woodlands, smell its fragrance,

as I see crystalline light dance midst the delicate
floral gatherings of May, and my tears drop
stepping carefully so as not to crush

what rises before me, reflecting on these
memories, gentle recollections of a Swedish
flower and her *muguet*.

Lily of the Valley

Beneath soil, a colony confers;
it networks and stirs, spreads
lifelines within sandy huddles
of darkness. Here, rhizomes root

with cool aplomb till shoots
emerge to collect spring sun.
When, petite buds open
on flowering stems—white

skirts adorned, curl-flourish
on hems. And, a sweet scent rises
with subtle bouquet, May Bells
thrive laced in poisonous array.

A Wood Thrush Sings

High in the treetop,
under summer's
emerald umbrella,
a wood thrush sings.

His languor of note,
flutelike and spare,
drops gently, while dusk
washes the woodlands,

moving afternoon's
last blush of light
toward horizon's
crimson slumber.

Heavy Things

small
robust

cool alloy
weighted beacon

beckons
talismans take

many shapes
today its form

a paperweight
half-pint hands

hold
embrace

heavy things
to soothe

abate
quell the tempest

ballast calm
metal magic

in her palm

II. Dimmer Switch

North American Robin

You arrive
one day before
this equal night

before sun
and earth attune.
You land

on cool ground
eager to feed
breed

break new ground
to build nests
lay clutches

of blue
tend
to your young.

And when
you tend
you'll be vigilant

as you scan
for snake
and squirrel

dive-bomb
blue jay and crow
guard

against grackle
until you tire
and when you do

hawk will come.
She'll take you
with curved talons

then stand
on warm ground

stained
with the silence
of your song.

Brule, in June

Rest a while
just sit
notice the air
each touch
tickle
rouse spruce
flutter fern
send sumac
to shudder.
And listen
as thrush
and thrasher
awaken
the woodlands
enliven
their home
with drills
trills
spilling notes
of musical
flourish. So
rest a while
just sit
memorize
these moments
freeze them

for December
breathes
in every
Brule breeze
of June.

Transition,
On the Day He Died

Bedridden and pale, but
still with pursuit, he faced
the window and searched

through panes marked by
frost's touch—morning's
mirth authored lacework,

rime written in silver
plated on glass. Winter's
verse rendered respite,

interlude, from cancer's
curse, invited insight,
bid pause to visions rising,

buds pushing, purple
reaching for March skies.
All day he gathered crocus,

though they lie dormant
awaiting rebirth. It was
dead of night when his

bones lifted. He steadied
himself, planted both feet,
rose and proclaimed,

Jeannie E. Roberts

The pain is gone. I can walk.
Then he pushed past crocus,
beyond March skies, and into
the light.

Ides of March, 1972

October's death sat fresh
until January's hit. February's
was expected, though shocking
nonetheless. And March's?
It went something like this:

after pall of malignancy
seized his being and daybreak
sank into terminal silence,
numbness hushed her internal
bloom. Death played dominoes.
Daughter followed Father; they
fell sequentially, cancelling
each other out.

Predators

*We don't protect our young, and we tolerate
predators of our own species.*
—Andrew Vachss, American Writer

North of nowhere

down rock roads

east to yesterday

first stars hold

wide-eyed wishes

and heads turn

all smiles and teeth

for pretty girls

girls naive

to biting ways

girls sweet

to those who sink

wounds into wishes

that start with stars

north of nowhere

down rock roads

east of yesterday.

Arctic

You stretch
before me

featureless
frozen

flat
amid

your rigid
nature

your vast
ocean of ice.

Your grave
horizon

abates
mosses

and grasses
lessens

lichens.
You bridle

your tundra
with frigidity

kin to the cold
hold of husbands

who wield wives
in matrimony.

She Walks

When trinkets
turn savvy
and trophies
break mold
when beauty
spikes envy
and gossip
takes hold
when vision
lacks insight
and falsehoods
mask truth
when smiles
feign kindness
and rudeness
crowds couth
when secrets
shape families
and darkness
rules lives
when grudges
grow stronger
and husbands
cheat wives
she walks
she walks
she walks into
the light.

Miscarriage

you left home

slipped away

a mere bud

a whisper

in white

perhaps

you passed

through

altered time

beheld

a better place

took root

in brighter space

thrived

in a finer womb

after your heart

set my heart

abloom

Rattles

—for Brother

a rattlesnake's
tail can
sustain
its shake
for nearly
three hours

like a pit
viper's
warning
his death
rattle shook

air hissed
and
wheezed
until this
knocking
sound
stopped

with loss
of rattle
she cried
like a baby
shaken
once more
by death

Birdbath

Tonight, you chat as you splash,
so pleased to break away,
away from the thicket,
beyond branches and brush,

far from the forest
and the tiresome back and forth,
to this basin. Your bib beads
with water, your black cap drips

as you dip, and while you bathe,
your body pitches with pleasure.
Dee-dee-dee, you whistle.
Your feathers flutter, carefree

you call, *chick-a-dee-dee-dee!*
Tonight, you escape
gaping beaks
for a moment or two.

Traveling with Tree Frog and the Two-Wheeled Sport Warrior

Riding the lip
crossing streets
bridges
escorting the past
and its rickety
transport
ashen bonds
adhere
near legs
of mahogany
and oak
cling
beside the turn
and spindle
of a lineage
lost.

Like tree frog
she rides greyly
fused
to this trailer
this hearse
of ragged
remains.
Having hauled
for decades

she's keen
on release
her elegy
word-less
her lamentation
spent.

And what
have you learned
from your crouch
and camouflage
this graying
heaviness?
To restore
your verdant
nature

and lightness
to drop
this drag?

Tree Frog

Where it's cool
against my skin,
I remain

unnoticed,
hidden inside
shroud, within

shadow, tucked
tightly away,
atop bark,

below branch.
You could say,
I've dressed

for dinner—
donned
dust-colored

cloak, daubed
in drab
with a tincture

of taupe.

In time,
I'll expose

my brilliance—
change
to my favorite

shade of green.
But until then,
I'll pose

near spider,
posture by fly,
then leap

to the occasion,
knife and fork
in hand.

Last Call

The last lilt of summer glints
with frills of pampas poised
near sedums' mauve stance
with mushrooms' pallid caps
buttoned between acorns
and undergrowth of oak
with the skitter of squirrels
midst dappled slides
of silken light.

September calls
with sounds of tree frogs
the soft ring of crickets
the lonesome hover
of hummingbird
over canine's
slumberous sighs
as lone daisy leans
her yellow goodbyes.

The Punctuation
of Ferns

Like snail shells
nestled in crooks
of question marks,

fiddleheads coil,
cap fronds, within
ponds of noonday sun.

Spirals unfurl, respond
without question, roll
out the answer, clarify

meaning in the fleeting
nature of time; only
to rest, repose, after

accentuating glens,
underlining gullies,
hyphenating ditches

with dashes of green,
upon making their mark,
completing this seasonal

sentence, before fading
to full stop and finishing
with periodic ending points.

Observations Bring Hope on an April Day

—in memory

Near bracts and stalks, along the fade
and wilt of cattails, buffleheads float
past the stems and remnants that hem
this pond, dive midst the subtle shine
of slate-colored waters, blur beside
stands of withered remains where
sequined light capers beyond the traces
that embody a season of leavings. Here
in prismatic greens and purples, drakes'
crests shine—their plumage reflects
in spills of black and white as mates
blend in feathered waves of grayness.

Midst the graying wilt of my heart,
where loss stalks, blurs beside a season
of leavings, I stand near the shining spill
of ducks and I'm reminded of spring—
how the stirrings of Earth crest green
and the journeys of birth crown purple,
how dawning's trace every stem,
embody each remnant in prismatic
waves of abiding light—its legacy rises,
in luscious intervals, in the gracious giving
of existence.

III. Natural Orbits

Gathering Blossoms

> *Where will you plant your grief-seeds? We need ground*
> *to scrape and hoe, not the sky of unspecified desire.*
> —Rumi

Loss rose from her garden,
spoke gently between plantings,

conversed softly of death
and dianthus, of despair and dahlias.

Guided by grief, heart in dust,
mind in memory, tears fell, sank,

into the loam of soul. Each turn
of hoe, every scrape into ground,

became honorable labor, honorable
in its intention to transform.

Digging, unearthing, seeing,
she beheld her father, followed

his image as he tended to tea rose
and tulip, dianthus and dahlia;

she watched his eyes brighten
as he handled, cupped, the stuff of life.

Buried in darkness, stirrings
pushed where seedlings emerged,

where buds reached for the sky, grew
with the specified desire to live!

Blossoms rose from her garden;
they swirled in crinolines of green,

delighted in bonnets of petalled-softness,
as if to say, *Dance with us, laugh,*
we're your grief-seeds—transformed!

Swedish Flooring

The old linoleum spoke,
kept track, took note,
of scuffs and cracks,
marked anecdote, recalled
a lifetime worn by others;
where, thoughts of feet
made floorboards creak,
caused stabs near grab
of knob and turn meant
throbs when dotard trod
with memory-mud and
gore; still, shine imbued
in servitude, light infused
this floor, where pets were
friends, pledged care—no end,
and softness sat times four, sat
just beyond the door.

Shades

It's Autumn now
and overhead
ponderosas pitch,
weave with whites'
rusty flushed needles
and shades of malachite
mix amid spruce
and cedar, their
crimped and crooked
leaders aim skyward,
angle beside birch
and maple, here
branches left bare,
bereft, serve as perch,
scaffold, for sparrow
and wren. She heeds
this line of October
pine as her crimped
and crooked fingers
perch, poise themselves,
on Pentel, letter left to right
across rules of blue
on yellow. And solace
ascends this rusty flushed
evening in shades of mauve
and malachite.

Pomes, fruit produced by flowering plants

On fall mornings,
we'd watch them flock.
Hundreds gathered,

gorged themselves
on the red,
berry-like fruit

from the *pyracantha*.
Autumn brought
ripeness and robins

to pomes. Pomes,
fleshy and fermented,
sodden with rime,

filled beaks
with bitter
but blissful doses

of sugar alcohol.
Feeling lyrical
and light, robins

strived for flight
but staggered,
stumbled,

alliterated the lawn
in laggard lines
of loaded stanza.

And robins
wrote poems.

Being October

She whispers
speaks softly
in hushes
hints
of honey
breaths
of blush
and russet
as sighs
of wine
imbue
her limbs
infuse
her bounty
in florid
bouquet.
Stippled
in light
she bathes
beside
amber
sways
before
coral
sweeps
abreast
salmon

leaving
traces
of color
gracing
her reign
surrendering
as an autumn
abandons its crown
for she is October
the quintessential ten.

Fresh Corduroy

Branches bow
with morning snowfall

Needles net
crystals alight

Snow draws
an artist's outline

Winter sets
its stage at night

Voices travel
in pine forest

Skiers stride
on trails of white

Weight shifts
to gain momentum

Poles plant
from left to right

Skis glide
with ease of motion

Patterns form
imprints unite

Sun paints
a coral canvas

Shadows sweep
to meet twilight

Dark falls
upon horizon

Stars unveil
the skies ignite

Sleep calls
to early risers

Groomers wake
to work at night

Bully breaks
nocturnal silence

Pistons churn
by soft moonlight

Paths combed
with surface rhythm

Corduroy shines
in dawn's first light

Branches bow
with morning snowfall

Needles net
crystals alight

Voices travel
in pine forest

Skiers stride
on trails of white

Writing, in Winter

These days endure
like attic webs, like
field corn forgotten,
like snoring dogs.
Where focus sojourns
out a window, pauses
for a sip of tea, wanders
with an Asian beetle.
Time hangs cobwebs
and distracted poets
like me.

After Surgery

Her cane hangs beneath hovering wings.
She favors distraction and this circus
for a drink—the whir, the hum, the sum
of aerial antics. And, for a moment
they're one, poised in silhouette,
yet, all aflutter for flight. Where
she sees herself as bird, butterfly
or moth, thirsty for the whir, the hum
of health aloft; still, she's mindful
of her veil, this convalescent cloth—
some days slow like snail, and others
still like sloth.

March

Snow bows,
yields,
lightens
its lading,
releases
its grip,
gently flows.
Melt bathes,
soaks,
verdantly
aiding
new growth,
season's surge.
Bird fans,
lands, rests
abreast briar,
rouses
its crier-like
call, *Cheer!*
Cheer! Spring's
nearly here!
Sun blazes
toward April.
March thaws.

Coffee Table

Something sounds
at your base; its
noise is deafening:
teeth and chain,

choke and throttle.
Bark flies—hits
aspen, wounds alder.
You tip and crash,

trunk to ground, where
your rings reveal
a much older growth,
an elder among oak.

Your fate? A holder
among men, a flat-top
for beer. And did you say
a coaster, my dear?

The Matinee

Scent of sap
and needle
sate the chase
perfume pursuits
that trace jungles
gyms
of limb
and timber.

Feet scurry
scamper
round riggings
of twigs
land balanced
on beams
seize branches

where sparks stir
and flurry settles
just long enough
for gray squirrels
to mate.

Firefly

In the curves of this valley
where oaks and pines meet
where moon shines and moss
softens as day creatures sleep
sirens stalk.

Coleoptera cruise
coal-black night
mimic mating signals
cast lures of cold light

femme fatales flash
fly for the feast
where female *photuris*
attracts kills then eats

in the curves of this valley
where oaks and pines meet
where the glow of death lingers
as summer's soul and heart beats

Jeannie E. Roberts

My Church

Over afternoon
shadows,
dragonfly darts.

Wild cucumber's
wiry vine
climbs sumac.

Ferns burgeon
beneath birch;
their fronds veil

to vole and moss.
Ponderosa,
spruce, white

rise before me
as stitches of light
seam between

needles. In this
cathedral of boughs
cardinal call

and oriole orange
are alms, a glowing
choir warbling

aloft branches
that line, design
panels of sky.

And filigreed hues
seep through
nature-made

stained glass—
framing rose,
peach, plum,

the sum
of sundown
and this day's
benediction.

Rush River Fish

Minnows glisten

hasten
past crayfish

slip
along rapid's

ripple, rise
within

current's surge
glide

amid
liquid realms

one body
one school

en masse
downstream

Tom Boy

Unshod
near water's edge
breezes
touch tresses
trace locks
of copper
and chestnut;
strands stir
share the air
with sedges
buoy
beside cattails.

Steeped
in summer
feet ooze
sink
with sunset
roam barefoot
beyond bulrush
in the dimming
flush
of twilight
and back
toward home.

Oddly Enough

It awakens
unequaled.
Shades lift

with peerless
might. Singular
in its journey

to disperse
distinctive light.
Alone

on Earth's horizon
unmatched
in its display

detached
from all things
common

from mans'
mere mortal
ways.

Release

—October 16, 2014

She lives in mist, she lives
in moon, where starlit nights
display. She lives near banks,
where currents turn, where
river's rush is cradled,
where wilderness resides.
She lives near cliffs, where
swallows nest, where ferns
and trees abide. She lives
in Earth, where birth endures,
where permanence survives.
She lives through love,
in eyes that tear, in hearts
that gently pray, where songs
along Stonehammer lift this dust-
divining day.

Because Nice Matters
(or does it?)

After a lifetime of pleasantries and politeness, rarely crossing the line, smiling down the nice-nelly path to nowhere, before age, dementia and death swallowed my mother, she stepped back. She stepped back for Dad. Mom was his backdrop, the background to his foreground, the consent to his control. In her mid-eighties she told me, I'm sorry I raised you girls to be nice. Though liberating to hear, I'd learned long ago that being a nice person only encouraged others to take advantage, to use, to assign labels like pushover or easy target. Knowing this, I'd still slip into its vortex while hearing these internal calls: be a good girl now, know your place, mind your manners, if you don't have something nice to say, say nothing at all! Mom's apologetic words freed my voice, gave me the permission to write this (not-so-nice) piece by choice.

Birth

Let egg
embryo
germ

and
generation

descent
and
derivation

root
in the source
of her origin

let seed
stem
well

ripen
until

her life-force
unshackles
from shell.

Notes

I. Holding Moments

"Along the Old Abe State Trail": Old Abe State Trail refers to a 19.5
mile multi-use paved rail trail in Chippewa County, Wisconsin, USA.
Buffleheads (*Bucephala albeola*) are small American sea ducks. Chippewa
refers to the Chippewa River.

"Front Porch": the forgiveness quote is often attributed to Mark Twain,
but there is no substantive evidence that this is correct.
Similar context has appeared by the following writers: Sophia May
Eckley, Ella A. Giles, Elizabeth Reeves Humphreys,
George Roemisch, and others.

"When Barred Owls Broadcast": Hallie or Lake Hallie is a village
in Chippewa County, Wisconsin, USA. *Strix varia* is the binomial,
scientific or Latin name for barred owl. Strix identifies its genus and varia
identifies its species within the genus.

"Berry Picking" and "Art Fair": Pepin and Stockholm are villages within
Pepin County, Wisconsin, USA. Great River Road (Highway 35) is a
Wisconsin state highway running north-south across western Wisconsin,
USA.

"*Muguet*": Kosta Boda is a brand of Swedish crystal. This glassworks
company was founded in Kosta, in the Swedish province of Småland, in
1742.

II. Dimmer Switch

"Brule, in June": Brule refers to a town in Douglas County, Wisconsin, USA. The town takes its name from the nearby Bois Brule River.

"Ides of March, 1972": the Ides of March corresponds to the 15th day of March on the Roman calendar. It also refers to the death of Julius Caesar in 44 BC and its subsequent transition period. The death referred to within this poem occurred on March 18th.

"Predators": Andrew Vachss is a crime fiction author, child protection consultant, and attorney representing children and youth. He is also an advocate against animal abuse.

III. Natural Orbits

"Gathering Blossoms": the Rumi quote was taken from *The Soul of Rumi*, by Coleman Barks, Harper San Francisco, 2001, page 32.
Jalal ad-Din Muhammad Rumi was a 13th-century Persian poet, scholar, and Sufi mystic.

"Shades": Pentel refers to a brand of mechanical pencil.

"Pomes, fruit produced by flowering plants": *Pyracantha* refers to the scientific classification for a genus of large, thorny evergreen shrubs in the Rosaceae family.

"Fresh Corduroy": Fresh corduroy refers to the pattern the snow forms after a pistenbully (bully) has groomed the ski trails. The snow's surface becomes finely ridged, resembling corduroy material.

"Firefly": *Coleoptera* refers to the scientific classification for an order of insects commonly called beetles. *Photuris* refers to the scientific classification for a genus of fireflies (beetles of the Lampyridae family), including the femme fatale lightning bugs of North America.

"Rush River Fish":   refers to the valley with river near the unincorporated town of Martell, in Pierce County, Wisconsin, USA.

"Release": Stonehammer refers to the name of the Rush River property with rock cliff near the unincorporated town of Martell, in Pierce County, Wisconsin, USA.

Acknowledgments

My thanks to the editors of the following books, anthologies, and periodicals in which some of the poems, sometimes in slightly different versions, have previously appeared.

Blue Heron Review (online poetry magazine): "Observations Bring Hope on an April Day."

Cross Country Skier Magazine | The Journal of Nordic Skiing: "Fresh Corduroy."

Deepening Engagement | *Essential Wisdom for Listening and Leading with Purpose, Meaning and Joy* (Skylight Paths Publishing): "Gathering Blossoms."

father's and what must be said (Rebel Poetry): "Gratitude" (formerly titled "What my Father Said").

Festival of Language's *Festival Writer* (online literary journal): "Arctic," "Pomes, fruit produced by flowering plants," "Traveling with Tree Frog and the Two-Wheeled Sport Warrior."

Goose River Anthology (Goose River Press): "Art Fair."

Little Eagle's RE / VERSE (online blogspot): "Butterfly," "The Punctuation of Ferns."

Misty Mountain Review (online literary journal): "Along the Old Abe State Trail," "Butternuts," "Four-Leafing at Age Eight," "Tree Frog."

Nature of it All (poetry chapbook, Finishing Line Press): "A Wood Thrush Sings," "Birdbath," "Butterfly," "My Church," "The Punctuation of Ferns."

Off the Coast (Resolute Bear Press): "After Surgery."

Peninsula Pulse | resource for the arts, news & entertainment (online): "Firefly," "The Matinee," "When Barred Owls Broadcast."

Quill & Parchment (online literary journal): "A Wood Thrush Sings," "Being October," "My Church" (formerly titled "Church, in Summer"), "Front Porch," "Tom Boy."

The Blue Max Review (Rebel Poetry): "Last Call."

The Moon Magazine (online literary journal): "Birth," "Release."

The Poetry Storehouse | great contemporary poems for creative remix (online): "Birth," "*Muguet*," "Rattles," "Shades."

Three Minus One: Parents' Stories of Love & Loss (She Writes Press): "Miscarriage."

Verse Wisconsin (print and online literary journal): "Because Nice Matters (or does it?)," "Birdbath."

Volume One Magazine (print and online literary section): "Tom Boy."

Wisconsin Fellowship of Poets' *Wisconsin Poets' Calendar 2015*: "Brule, in June."

Wisconsin Fellowship of Poets' *Wisconsin Poets' Calendar 2014*: "Berry Picking."

Wisconsin Fellowship of Poets' *Wisconsin Poets' Calendar 2013*: "Rush River Fish."

Woodland Pattern's Blog │ dedicated to the discovery, cultivation and presentation of contemporary literature and the arts (online blogspot): "Oddly Enough."

Zingara Poet (online literary journal): "Swedish Flooring."

Zouch Magazine & Miscellany (online journal): "North American Robin."

Jeannie E. Roberts lives in an inspiring rural setting near Chippewa Falls, Wisconsin. She is the author of *Nature of it All*, a poetry chapbook (Finishing Line Press, 2013), and the author and illustrator of *Let's Make Faces!*, a children's book (Rhyme the Roost Books, an imprint of JR Creative Studios, 2009). Born in Minneapolis, Minnesota, her work appears widely in print and online literary journals and anthologies. She draws, paints, and often photographs her natural surroundings. Learn more about Jeannie at www.jrcreative.biz.

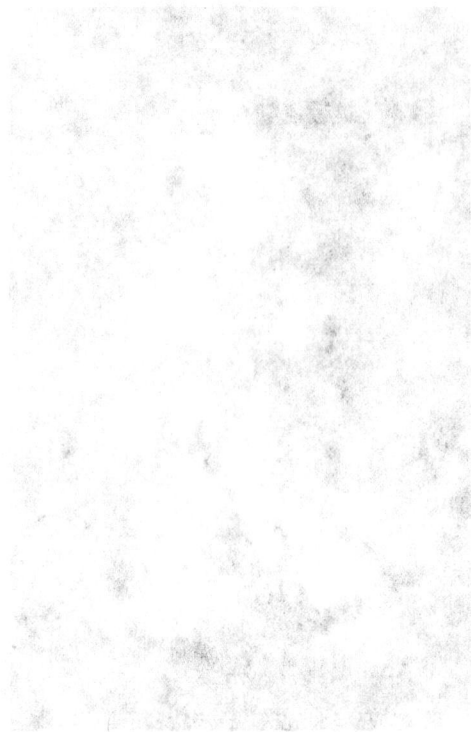

www.ingramcontent.com/pod-product-compliance
Lightning Source LLC
Chambersburg PA
CBHW062103270326
41931CB00013B/3198